CLIMATE CHANGE

CLIMATE CHANGE

Consciousness Change

Translated By

Carla R. Mancari

Celestial Literary Group

The contents of this book are not meant to take the place of qualified medical professionals or therapists. There is no expressed or implied guarantee regarding the effects of the suggestions or the liability taken.

CONTENTS

ACKNOWLEDGMENTS

I am grateful to all the individuals involved in climate change. They bring different points of view worth considering.

My sincere thanks to all healthcare providers addressing the effects of an ailing environment on our health.

I am grateful to the environment's active protectors and authors who have written and are writing to sound the alarm for the silent voice of an ailing environment.

It is my sincere hope that we can all hear the ringing and see a little more clearly the health threat and the environment's need for each one of us to come to its aid.

Thanks to Mary Carpenter for reviewing and editing the manuscript. Not an easy task.

INTRODUCTION

"Climate change" has almost become a dirty phrase. It induces arguments among family members and friends and is a political bouncing ball among many politicians. But in this work, climate change and the environment are treated as the same. Climate change, good or bad, causes environmental changes.

Climate Change: Consciousness Change does not take sides in the climate change debate. Taking sides would only prolong the solution to what many consider, or may not consider, a serious problem. *Climate Change: Consciousness Change* does offer a solution. It is a solution that hopefully all sides of the issue may agree upon, work with, and move on.

A review of your Spiritual Center and the Minute Meditation is included, which takes you on an adventurous journey. It reviews awareness, energy, consciousness, mind, and the effects of conditioning. It enables you to take charge and advocate for climate change and your well-being.

You will learn how to clean up your interior environment while living in harmony with your outer environment. The stories included are either ones I have created or ones I have heard many times from different teachers, masters, and gurus. Therefore, it is impossible to assign credit to any individual for originality.

This is a one-of-a-kind solution to transforming yourself, your living space, and the world. *Climate Change: Consciousness Change* is offered for the welfare of the environment *and* your health. It is backed by more than forty years of practice, which has been shared with many groups and individuals.

1

CLIMATE CHANGE
The Three Sides

Climate Change is a three-sided issue. There are those who believe in it, those who do not, and those who have not decided what they believe. Climate change is a problem for all three sides because it continues to divide the nation. Compromise, consensus, or an acceptable solution does not appear on the immediate horizon.

You can beat an issue to death. This issue, however, seems unwilling to die. And it has and continues to take a horrendous beating. Why?

Climate change affects the environment. Let's face it, is there any issue more life-connected than our environment? It is not a question of our survival but how we survive. Working with the symptoms will not solve the issue. The need is to understand the cause and to be aware of what it is you want.

Do you want a healthier life? Do you want a more stress-free life? Given a choice, would you trade health for wealth? It's the poorest trade-off. Poor physical and mental health consequences exist for the billions who depend on this planet for life.

You are one of the billions. Your physical and mental health is endangered. A deteriorated environment *is* a deteriorated you. Your saving the environment from destruction is saving you from destruction.

Many environmental organizations exist, including churches, schools, states, and the federal government. These organizations translate into millions of individuals interested in climate change and the environment. There are enough organizations and agencies spouting "solutions" to fill the Grand Canyon. There is a need for National support for the solutions. Unfortunately, the current political climate does not lean that way.

If individual consciousness within a Nation is not stirred, the National collective consciousness stagnates. Our great Nation is capable of getting the job done. Your consciousness must be clean from the inside. The outer environment reflects your inner One (chapter 6 – Consciousness Change, Climate Change).

An online search for "environmental issues" produced 778,013,447 results and listed more than 230 countries with environmental risks of every kind. Don't you hate statistics? I do. I find environmental articles and books to be both enlightening *and* depressing. It's easy to become overwhelmed by the horrendous bad news and opposing views.

Climate change is a popular subject that is going nowhere. Your consciousness contributes to your health problems and to environmental endangerment. There are oil spills, nuclear crises, air and water pollution, and rising ocean levels. How might these situations be different if everyone involved focused on benefiting their health and the ecosystem?

You can be sensitive to the health of your loved ones and to your own health. You can be sensitive to that which feeds you, quenches your thirst, clothes you, provides the air you breathe, and shelters you from the elements. It's up to you to care.

Although *Climate Change: Consciousness Change* dares to prick your conscience, it is user-friendly. It is not intended to do harm but to help you to avoid harming yourself. Many individuals are hurrying to get on the green bandwagon. You can help steer it in the right direction. Unfortunately, you may be one of the many affected by climate change. *Climate*

Change: Consciousness Change's solution may help break the cycle of an addicted, conditioned consciousness.

In a chaotic world, a positive solution to what ails you and the environment may make a difference in your health and daily life. You may choose to be a power of one or a lifetime of health problems. It is a minor investment with significant returns.

2

MOTHER
EARTH

A Visit With Mother Earth

Mother Earth's nature is to supply unlimited resources. Her only purpose is to meet and support your every need. Can you hear the silent voice (the condition) of Mother Earth? There is a silence so loud it can be heard. Look around you, and you may realize a silent language that speaks to you. You may come to understand this language more easily than any language in this world.

True, the voice of Mother Earth is silent, but her outcry can be seen in human diseases and Mother Earth's environment's appearance of deterioration and neglect. Her loudest cry and the most painful effects of climate change come from your pretense that all is well. As a child, you were more receptive to the silent voice of Mother Earth than to those who would mold you into their image. You tumbled on her grass, stepped into her mud puddles, and climbed her trees. You constantly were embracing Mother Earth.

Just imagine what Mother Earth would have to say if she could audibly speak to you today. Would you hear her? Visit with her, and then listen carefully. She doesn't mix her words.

~~

"Hi, Mama, how are you? You look troubled."

Her voice suggests a rising tidal wave. *"Who in the hell are you?"* You stare in disbelief. How could she not know you?

"I'm one of your billions of kids."

She cantankerously replies, *"That is nothing to brag about. Where have you been?"*

Your courage is silently tumbling down. *"Well, I'm all grown up and have a family of my own to look after."*

"Damn, you are dumb. Just who do you think grew you up? Food from my lands, water from my rivers, shelter from my forest, and that is just for starters."

Mama is in her element now. Every word comes down upon you with ten lashes. You apologetically plead your case.

"Oh yeah, sure, but I am busy taking care of my family. This discussion about climate change is too time-consuming, and you know, Mama, I do have to work for a living."

"Wow! Twice dumb."

Now Mama Earth isn't holding back. She is really upset.

"What did I raise, an idiot? It's still your Mama Earth who is providing for you and your family. As for work, do not give me any of your intellectual jargon. You would not have a job if I didn't supply the materials. Technology is worthless without the materials to implement it. Get a little smarts, why don't you?

"Besides, none of you kids work as hard as your Mama. Just look at the environment I've provided for you. Then, look at the condition climate change has put it in."

You fumble for the right words from the darkness that overshadows you. *"But Mama, you've got to understand. These are different times. There are so many demands on my time."*

An indignant Mama shouts, *"I GOT TO UNDERSTAND?"* Then toning it down, she retorts, *"The only difference now is there are more of you kids to feed and clothe, more of you to house and water, and more of you demanding more of my resources.*

"One Mama takes care of billions of her kids, but the billions of kids can't take care of one Mama? Child, are you that stupid or taking me for a fool?"

Inhaling a deep gulp of air, you apologetically assure her, *"Oh no, Mama, I would never do that. I am here, aren't I? I just want to know how you are doing. No reason to be so distraught about it."*

"Bingo! Dumb times three. You got your head up your butt? Or are you just jerking me around? Look at me; I'm constantly battered about, taking blows and verbal insults."

You seem like an absurd, pathetic creature. You attempt to re-engage Mama Earth.

"These are difficult times for all of us. True, I have neglected you, but . . ."

"Neglected me? Boy, you are irredeemably stupid. You damn well are destroying me. Yet, I continue to feed the very fire that con-

*sumes me. You inconsiderate bunch of bana-
nas."*

Impotently, you crawl back to your intellectual hole, and you know Mama Earth is
infected with the darkness of rejection and de-
spondency.

*"Okay, okay, Mama, I get the picture, but
you have not always been cooperative either.
What with hurricanes, floods, and . . ."*

*"Are you telling me I am hurting you? You
piss in the air; you're gonna get wet."*

~~

Mama's words cut like a sharp razor.
What did she know that you did not? With a
mind flushed with sadness, Mother Earth is not
deluded into thinking things will eventually
change. She is deserted. It is a gloomy atmos-
phere.

I believe we all get the message here.
We are responsible for Mother Earth's environment. But we are not doing an excellent job
of caring for it. In 1993, author Harold W. Bernard Jr. warned that the wolf was beyond
knocking at our door. He questioned how many
people have listened to what our world tells us.

In our century, the wolf has taken up permanent residence. It is the unwanted guest who came for a few days and stayed. As you learn to listen to the silent voice of Mother Earth, your inner hearing deepens—insights and wisdom are realized. Look around you, and you will hear the silent voice of Mother Earth crying out for you to come to her environment's rescue.

3

CONDITIONING
The Cause

Right up front, let us get to the cause of climate change. Climate change is a symptom. It is a symptom of how you think, speak, and act. So, what is there that influences the way you think, speak, and act? Conditioning!

Conditioning is the cause of your thoughts, words, and actions. Through repetition, conditioning is accomplished with labels, names, and identities given to persons, objects, feelings, thoughts, and emotions. As a conscious being, you have a mind, thoughts, and senses—hearing, taste, touch, sight, and smell—which have a natural power to receive impressions through the body organs. The thoughts and impressions are stamped with the conditioning of the culture or society you live in.

You are conditioned in thought, word, and deed from the moment you enter this world of opposites. Conditioning is continually being done by parents, friends, peers, authority figures, and politicians. Your moral judgment is based on the conditioning of what is considered right or wrong, good or bad, according to an established culture, religion, and political parties.

Because shapes and forms of objects are constructed for use, you are conditioned to think of and see their practical use rather than realize their essence. For example, a block of wood cut from a tree, then carved into a chair or table, is always seen and thought of as a chair or table. However, it remains the wood (tree/seed), and if it were burned, it would be ashes. Therefore, the chair or table is only a functional concept of its reality. Thus, abuse of our environment takes a hit.

When using conscious sight and thought, you see and think "chair, or "table." You are not purely seeing. You see a concept. If you are not in a state of pure consciousness, your belief is in the conditioned consciousness of sense impressions

Conditioning creates practical, functional labeled concepts (such as a chair or table) for communication and identifying objects and individual beings. It may also create false concepts of thought patterns and sense impressions. False concepts are created when you accept the appearance of anything (or anyone) as its reality. Conditioning may create a false sense of self, separate and apart from the spirituality of your being and your relationship with the environment.

From the time you are born, your conscious mind and the physical body are given a name. Repeatedly hearing your mind and body addressed with the given name causes you to identify with it as who you are. You are taught the use of I, me, my, and mine, which become personal attachments to the name. All are concepts; none is the reality of who you are.

The entire package of conditioned mind, thoughts, and physical body is a sense impression that leads you to falsely identify as a separate personal being, which you are not. From this kind of thinking comes a lack of appreciation for the environment that provides the materials to create the concepts you use. As you abuse and misuse your environment, causing climate change, you refuse to accept responsibility for your actions. You are related to all human beings *and* the environment, but because of personal conditioning, a disconnect exists. Now you may understand the cause of climate change.

Let us take it a step further. Ultimately, I am talking about the conditioning of consciousness. So, you need to review awareness, energy, and consciousness because Awareness, energy, and consciousness are what you and the environment are made of.

4

**AWARENESS
ENERGY
CONSCIOUSNESS**

Awareness

Awareness is calm, silent, subtle, and changeless. The mind cannot grasp awareness. Attempting to understand your awareness of your being with the conscious mind is an exercise in futility. The mind cannot grasp that which is beyond it.

You cannot be conscious of awareness. Awareness has no self-reflection, no self-identity. Awareness has no opposites, no separate sense of a personal being.

Consciousness-Energy

Consciousness, in general, is vibrating energy that causes many varied manifestations in the world. The different frequencies of vibrating energy are continually changing. Energy has been defined as positive or negative. It is the *use* of it that creates the negative or positive.

As you progress on your spiritual journey, you may become consciously aware of these changing, vibrating frequencies within your states of consciousness. You may be aware of the negative energy effect when you are aggravated or tired. The positive may be experienced as a high energy level when you are joyful, and your work performance is high without becoming tired. You are continually changing the frequency of your states of consciousness.

With a silent meditation practice (chapter 14), you may go beyond mind-and-body consciousness. Then, as you again become conscious of the mind and body, the consciousness of a separate personal "I" rises. The fact that you may go beyond the mind and body tells you that you are not the mind and body. You are not that which changes. You are not that which comes and goes. You are that which is permanent, changeless.

The different speeds/frequencies of your consciousness' energy vibration give a false sense of descending or ascending. There is just the awakening to the realization that you never went anywhere. You are where you began. Until you realize your true nature, you are a sleepwalker in a relative world of separate imaginary beings. When you realize your spirituality, you realize that in consciousness, you are not separate from other human beings *and* the environment's climate changes. The natural state of your being is love, love of self, love of all your individual manifested selves, and love for the environment that helps sustain you on the earth plane.

One Consciousness

There is One Consciousness expressing as the rising individual expressions of consciousness (not separate). Waking up to the One Consciousness removes the illusionary sense of many separate individuals. Within the One Consciousness, there are infinite "individual" expressions of consciousness, one of which is yours. Consciousness gives rise to many individual states of consciousness. Like the waves in the Ocean that arise from the Ocean depths, you are an individual but never separate or apart from the One Consciousness and your infinite source.

The Ocean's surface appears to have individual waves pounding the shore. Yet, in each wave exists the calm depth of the Ocean's water. Your consciousness's vibratory energy is much like Ocean waves. You can no more separate the One Consciousness from individual consciousness than you can separate the Ocean's depths from the individual waves.

It is within consciousness that the mind rises, and within the mind, a conscious sense of a physical body rises. It is the speed of the vibrating energy that determines the various conscious manifestations. The mind and its contents, thoughts, ideas, feelings with the senses, and sensations create a "sense" of a separate self-identity.

On this earth plane, the body, as an expression of consciousness' mind energy, vibrates at a slower speed. The slower vibrating energy frequency enables the body to appear, and it is sensed as a solid form. As you falsely identify with the mind, you falsely identify with a physical body separate from other individuals *and* the environment.

The false sense of a separate mind and body is the easiest vibratory energy to get attached to. The false sense of a separate personal body to defend, in fear of harm or death, may cause a perceptual gap challenging to venture beyond. You are constantly mixing, changing, and experiencing the different individual-expressed manifestations of consciousness. Conscious mind personalities can change/progress. Nothing on this earth plane is set in concrete.

There is no unmanifested consciousness. Whatever is within your expression of consciousness will eventually rise and manifest — that includes climate change or progress. You are never fixed on any individual expression of consciousness. Awakening to the truth of your spirituality is always available.

Truth may be realized with the practice of the silent Minute Meditation. A silent meditation practice creates space and may allow the rising of consciousness' contents. When seeking to realize the One Consciousness, you respect all manifesting individual expressions of the One Consciousness as you would respect your own.

As you sojourn through this world of life and death, you may have, through thought, word, and deed, misused (polluted) the purest of energy, causing negative climate change. This misuse of your One Consciousness' pure vibrating energy must be restored to its original purity. It is your responsibility to realize this and consent to its restoration. The silent Minute Meditation practice may purify the vibrating energy bringing an understanding of climate change with the least amount of time and effort.

When the One Consciousness is realized, you maintain and live out from a realized consciousness. To do otherwise is to insult your spiritual integrity. Therefore, you are always accountable whether you are living the life of a recluse or in this world of activity, you are responsible for climate change.

Once you have shattered self-identification with the separate false sense of mind and body, you have traveled beyond the false concepts which have held you captive. There is never a need to re-travel a road well worn. What has been realized in consciousness is ever-present. It is the ignorance of your spirituality that creates distortions and abuse of the environment. You may awaken to the realization that you are neither the body nor the mind. Yours is a greater reality. You are more, do not settle for less.

You have created the dreamer and the dream. Neither of which is the spirituality of who or what you are. You have identified with the dreamer and the dream — wake up and dream no more. Realize your spirituality. Real-

izing your spirituality may allow you to be consciously aware of the illusionary world of opposites and dissolve the denial of climate change.

During a silent Minute Meditation practice
(chapter 14), you are instructed to become
aware of your Spiritual Center *area* (chapter
12). If you are practicing with a determined
purpose, you may wake up to your spirituality
and your impact on climate change. You may
realize the earth's plane needs you.

5

THE
EARTH PLANE NEEDS
YOU

Do not Let It Down

The earth plane needs you. To argue that it does not is an exercise in futility. Of course, it needs you. Who else does it have? The earth plane needs every "you" it can get, but let us start with you.

Don't we all want to be needed by someone or something? Look no further. You are in the right place at the right time. Isn't it great to be needed?

True story: a huge, naked, crazy man stands on a corner and spits on individuals as they pass by. The locals consider him the town's fool and do their best to ignore him. One day, a rickshaw driver passes by, and the crazy man spits on him. The rickshaw driver then has his most profitable day ever. He tells his other fellow rickshaw drivers that he believes his good luck is because he was spat on that morning by the crazy fool. Sure enough, the following morning, rickshaw drivers are lining up to be spit upon. The moral of this story: the bigger the fool, the bigger the following.

Are you one who would quickly follow a fool? Obedience to individuals who would cause harm to the environment for their sake is blind obedience, which has no purpose and no progression. You are wiser than to give blind obedience to any individual. Blind obedience to such an individual may cause an emotional, internal conflict.

You are always in the now, and it is now that you are being asked to decide. Tomorrow's now may require a change, but todays now require a decision. How many "now's" have you struggled with that were indecisive? Perpetual indecision is an abusive relationship you have with yourself. Deciding that the earth plane needs *you* requires only one prerequisite—now. "Is my health important now? Will I contribute to the welfare of the earth's environment now?"

The decision placed on meeting the environment's needs makes a difference to your health and the health of your family and friends. They, too, are participants in the environment's riches. No outer pressure will make you realize the environment's needs. Lord, there has been plenty of that. Time and effort are wasted on the notion, "Should I, or shouldn't I? Is it right, or is it wrong?" "Is climate change real or not?" Instead, do what is necessary.

As you depend on the air you breathe, the environment, in return, depends on you. Conjuring up excuses for neglecting the environment will not wash. The results of your intended or unintended misbehavior toward the environment will always leave telltale signs. All the "ifs" and "buts" are escape hatches that are used to avoid committing.

"Ifs and buts" may be the most frequent response heard from you when you are faced with an invitation to step up and be accounted for in the cause to help a friend in need—the environment. It is always, "If I just had the time, I would …." "But for other commitments I have, I would …." If, and buts are the perfect pair of intentional avoidance.

Ifs are always predicated on conditions, and buts seek a backdoor out. They both say, "I am not ready. I am not willing. I am not prepared. I will not take the time or make the effort to help." Ifs and buts fool no one, including you. They are mind games you can never win. Whenever you hear yourself using an "if or but," stop to ask yourself, "Why am I turning away from an invitation to make a difference?" Procrastinating to meet the need of climate change will not stop its damage to your health.

There are many ways to procrastinate and put off an opportunity to make a difference. There are always big or little chores to do, errands to run, or friends to meet. Anything to occupy your mind and time will do. You may be too tired, so there is always the promise, "I will get to it soon, if not now, later, if not today, tomorrow." You always can make 101 excuses for putting off what climate change needs from you, but rarely is there a good reason.

For the well-intentioned, procrastinating is an art form. The most conscientious individual may fall under its spell. You may be one who protests, "I just do not have an extra minute in my busy schedule to give to the needs of the environment." You have so much to do and so many places to go. However, you need only walk upon and through the environment to realize it needs your attention. There is busy work, and many distractions are vying for your attention.

When your priorities change, your procrastinating will stop. You pick and choose, and if you choose to neglect climate change, you lose. You lose an opportunity to give help where a great need for help exists.

You are a special, unique individual who is capable of doing whatever you decide. Do not shortchange yourself! No other can step up with your particular gifts, talents, and potential for caring about climate change.

You are the power of one who can accept that climate change needs you, *and* you need it. That which is held near and dear is valued and appreciated. Unless you can value and appreciate that climate change needs your help, you will step into the trap of less-deserving things getting your unequivocal appreciation for all that the environment does for you.

The help that climate change needs lies within you, where your energy has no weariness and cannot be thwarted. The inner work you do will be reflected in all you do in your practical daily life. You are here to make a difference. If the earth's environment is to support and improve your health and life, it needs all of the support it can get from you. Give it. The planet needs *you*. Don't let it down.

6

CONSCIOUSNESS CHANGE

Climate Change

Consciousness change is the power invested in the manifestations of the earth's plane of opposites. We tend not to realize that the entire Universe is in consciousness, ours. Individual expressions of the states of consciousness have the invested power to cause Universal changes. That includes climate change, for better or worse. As individual expressions of the One Consciousness, your thoughts, words, and deeds contribute to climate change. That includes earthquakes, tornadoes, and hurricanes.

Storms and Other Disasters

Most of the causes of climate change are attributed to inconsiderate, harmful actions committed against the environment by individuals, industry, and politicians. This is, of course, one of the many serious causes. The outer is a reflection of the inner. In our present political climate, the manifestations of violent crimes, earthquakes, tsunamis, wildfires, and tornadoes are to be expected.

This nation is a reflection of its consciousness. The anger and the negativity conditioned in consciousness must manifest. There is no unmanifested consciousness.

Racism, hate, lack of tolerance, and lack of love for each other is reproduced in the outer appearance of hurricanes, tornadoes, and violent crimes. You sow what you think in thought, word, and deed.

You cannot escape the laws of this earth plane of "as you sow, you also shall reap." Look about you. Be aware of what individual consciousness is manifesting. Continuing to bury your head in the sand will one day allow the waters of the ocean to wash over you, and you will drown.

It is not an act of God. It is the actions and thoughts of individuals who refuse to acknowledge climate change and whose consciousness is pouring negativity into the environment. As individuals become more steeped in negative thoughts, words, and deeds, the catastrophic events will multiply. A negative consciousness is a trash-producing machine. The more trash you put out, the more trash will be produced. You cannot solve this problem from the outside alone.

Somewhere in this great Nation of ours, there must arise a leader. A leader who will realize that this is a Nation founded in consciousness, and it is in consciousness that together we will solve climate change. Individual consciousness is not set in stone. Consciousness change is possible, and consciousness change *is* climate change. If we are to change the outer, we must begin with the inner. You must be willing to tune into what is causing climate change. You must be willing to see, hear, and respond to the wrath that climate change is visiting on the earth plane.

Both negative and positive climate changes result from individual expressions of consciousness. Nothing occurs in a vacuum. All is the result of thoughts, words, and actions. It is not just what you are doing that pollutes the earth plane, but also what you think, because from your thoughts come your actions.

The problem is that you may only be aware of your limited surroundings. You may believe that you can only affect that which you can see, hear, and touch. It is not so.

One individual expression of consciousness, yours, possesses the power of the One Consciousness. Much like a drop of the Ocean possesses all of the ingredients of the mighty Ocean. You are never unconnected from the many within the mighty One Consciousness. There is nowhere that you can hide from the One Consciousness because you are ultimately the One Consciousness.

Climate change and disasters of any kind arise from the negative actions you commit and the negative states of consciousness you indulge in through thoughts, words, and deeds. Individuals who hate humans because of the color of their skin, religion, or sexual orientation will create disastrous environmental changes. Negative energy produces and feeds on disasters.

The higher a nation's percentage of hate-expressing individuals, the greater and more frequent the disasters become. Because hate is the opposite of love, it does possess the power of love. Love manifests the positive; hate manifests the negative. The opposite is always in the opposite. There lies the environment's salvation.

7

PRINCIPLE OF SUPPLY

Law of Attraction

The environment doesn't ask you to step up to the plate and just hit a home run. It asks you to win the game. It asks you to join a team that starts with you. Words won't get the job done, and neither will good intentions. Besides, we all know what the road to hell is paved with.

~~

A pompous, self-righteous individual dies. When he arrives up there, he knocks at the pearly gates. Saint Peter, appearing in his splendor of brilliance, answers the call. Glancing at the man and eager to know why he is there, Saint Peter asks, *"What is it you want?"*

Indignantly, the man responds, "I *want* to come in."

Amazed, Saint Peter questions, *"Oh! Why is that?"*

In exhilaration, the man replies, *"It's beautiful here, so green, so well kept."*

"Yes." Saint Peter agrees with the man's assessment and adds, *"We are aware and appreciative of our environment. We work at taking care of it. What have you done about climate change that is affecting the Earth's environment?"*

He dismisses Saint Peter's implication, pleading, *"Well, you see it's like this. I've been busy with my family and work. You know how that is. Time just slipped away, and before I knew it, I was here. But be assured, I always had plenty of good intentions."*

Softly smiling, Saint Peter replies, *"Ah! You are looking for the other place. The road there is paved with good intentions."*

~~

All of the environment's resources are organized around the principle of meeting your needs. When you abuse the environment's resources, you are abusing yourself. This world is responsive to the spiritual principle of supply. All you have and all you will ever need exists in abundance. Houses, cars, food, money, etc., are all forms of supply. They are just a few of the items, but the supply *itself* is unlimited and always available for your need, not greed.

In an environment where climate change is ignored, the environment is mistreated, abused, and neglected. The supply forms may deteriorate and become of little use. How many times in your life have you even expressed sincere gratitude for the ground you walk on or the air you breathe? If green is not your favorite color, brown will be.

Whenever you express sincere gratitude, there is a tender but firm new resolve to *be* your best, to *do* your best. It is this new resolve that strengthens your commitment and deepens your connection to the environment. When expressed, gratitude is a sincere caring love for yourself and a tremendous, bountiful love for the environment. The Minute Meditation (chapter 13) may give you a greater appreciation for the environment's worth. You make a connection, and you do not break it.

Your inherent spiritual supply source exists in unmanifested abundance. Your consciousness does double duty. It manifests through the principle of supplying the environment's resources to provide for you. It is then responsible for caring for those manifestations. You may understand from this the relationship you have with the environment.

Your consciousness's supply is limitless in its un-manifested source state. It can never be depleted. It is always manifesting in various forms as conditions or objects. There is a tendency to think of supply only in terms of the forms and shapes it takes. These are only the outer appearances of supply.

The forms and shapes manifesting are reflections of *your* expression of consciousness. When an object appears in a mirror, its reflection is but an indication of what is appearing. The mirror reflects the appearance. The mirror may show various forms and shapes, but the mirror *itself* never changes. So, it is with the principle of supply.

No matter how many forms or shapes the supply manifests in to meet your needs, the supply *source* remains untouched, never depleted. Look around. This earth's environment can produce all you shall ever need. It is not the principle of supply that limits its manifestations. It is man's manipulation of the principle of supply.

When the purity of the environment is destroyed, the purity of the free-flowing supply principle is stifled. The spiritual principle of supply is your inherent nature, and you cannot be separated from it, but its usefulness can be disrupted. You are responsible for the supply you bring forth on this plane and, if need be, for restoring it to its original state.

The environment will serve you only as well as you are willing to serve it. Your satisfaction, happiness, and fulfillment in the environment reside in the gratitude of your inherent supply source. Possessions have a life of their own and seek to claim your life. The environment's resources are all yours to use, but they do not exclusively belong to you. A permanent claim to any part of the environment is false.

No part of the environment can be permanently owned. It exists for all individuals' proper use, which includes the animal kingdom. Although at times a relationship with the environment can be difficult to maintain, an inherent clause of ownership is not written into it. You are the creator of the forms your supply source manifests. Thus, you are accountable for the proper use of all your manifestations of supply. You need not deprive yourself of their use. It is the misuse that causes unnecessary hardships in your life and in the environment.

If climate change is ignored, it will disturb the environment: the environment will disturb you. The environment's condition affects your mental and physical well-being. When you protect the environment, you protect yourself. The

Minute Meditation (chapter 13) may help you to realize the principle of supply. It may allow you to realize lasting joy and peace in your life *and* bring peace to your relationships with others and the environment.

There are choices to be made in recognition of climate change. It is easy to err by placing more value on temporary personal desires. Your intention needs to be grounded in Oneness with your source of supply. As long as you believe you are separate from your source, you are capable of harming yourself and the environment. You are one with the ecological environment's system. To think you can cut yourself off from the environment would be to believe you could cut yourself off from the air you breathe. Not possible!

Giving in to the temptation to misuse or abuse your environment's source of supply is a risk not worth taking. Appreciate and accept the things of this world for what they are, gifts to be cared for *and* enjoyed. Your response will, then, be sincere gratitude rather than insatiable greed.

8

NEGATIVE SURROUNDINGS
Coarser – Slower Vibrations

Negative surroundings bring to light negative situations and the energy vibrations of individuals you may be immersing yourself in. When situations and individuals vibrate negative energy, it creates a climate that surrounds you with coarser/slower vibrations. If you are not alert to the situations and individuals who are experiencing and expressing negative vibrations, you may be seduced by depression, illness, and sadness. You may create more negativity around you.

You may be fine one moment, then pow! You are hit over the head with negativity that is difficult to escape. Whether you unintentionally drift into a surrounding of negative vibrations, the result is the same. You may be overshadowed and taken into a tunnel of darkness.

It is easy to be unaware of just how deeply you have absorbed the negativity that surrounds you. You may only be aware that there is a heaviness tugging at you, and sorrow rising. The temptation is to believe in it and to worship at its fleeting moments. It may cause you to strike out at others and the environment. Taking ownership of other individuals' negativity is a heavy burden to carry. It is not yours. Give it up.

The conscious awareness that you have drifted into negativity is the first step out of a tunnel of darkness. Understanding negativity for what it is, a brief appearance in an illusory world, is the second step, which is the light that guides you out of the tunnel, your light. Negativity has no permanent life. Why would you want to adopt it? Negativity is not your nature. Why would you want to express it? Negativity has no home of its own. Why would you want to give it one?

It is never an easy task to overcome the surrounding negativity, but you possess the power to do so; use it. Step up to the plate and turn those negative thoughts into positive ones. Always remembering that in the opposite is the opposite. Hold fast to the inner joy that is always yours in the free spirit of your being, so that negativity cannot penetrate. Stand still and rise above the negativity that may cloud your remembrance of a God that daily displays before you, *Its* wondrous work, your environment.

9

CONSEQUENCES
Effects of Human Behavior

Consequences result from your choices and decisions. You will find that the effects of your behavior may be felt in the form of positive or negative consequences. Consequences, positive or negative, are the result of your behavioral conduct in thought, word, and deed. Everything you do bears consequences. Subtle or obvious, consequences are inherent in every thought, word, and deed.

Consequences are not punishment. They are due process. Consequences are self-inflicted and result when operating within a set of rules, regulations, and laws. Do not confuse forgiveness with consequences. Forgiveness does not exclude consequences. Being forgiven does not excuse you from bearing the consequences of your behavior.

The rules and laws of society cause negative consequences when you choose to ignore or willfully break them. They are stringent depending on the breach. So, also, it is that natural compliance with the laws of the universe results in decisions made from a place of responsibility for self, others, *and* the environment.

The natural laws of the universe cannot be ignored or broken. To believe that you can harm the environment and there will be no price to pay is illusory. There are consequences.

10

A
ME-FIRST
ATTITUDE
A Self-Imposed Prison

A me-first attitude, fostered by priorities wrapped in personal, social, or political agendas, causes society to be at war with itself. Its victims – your health, the environment, and climate change – are held prisoners to whatever a me-first attitude's shadow casts. The Minute Meditation may help break you out of that prison.

Climate change may not be at the top of your list. It also may not be allowed to compete with ego-stroking projects. Would it not be better to preserve before destroying and save before wiping out?

The resources the environment provides for your life's support are for your enjoyment. The environment only asks that its resources be respected. It is a choice you must make. A change in consciousness, good or bad, may result in climate change.

When you are practicing the Minute Meditation (chapter 14), you may become consciously aware of the effects climate change has on your health and the environment's health. You won't dabble when deciding what's right or wrong. You will do what is necessary. You do what is appropriate for your health and the environment.

Be aware that a fence of steel-minded resistance is masterfully woven to keep your mind in a trash collection of denials. When you attempt to unload the trash bin, be prepared for the battle your mind will wage and the turbulence it may cause. Nothing has a more significant negative impact on your life and the environment than abandoning or discarding your responsibility for climate change. Your health and the environment suffer dire effects even when mistakes are made unintentionally.

Many climate change organizations have taken a lot of heat for their attempt to alert a world of denial trash-bin collectors. Almost everyone would agree that individual human behavior will have to change. However, individual consciousness must change before human behavior *does* change.

11

CHANGE
OF
MIND

The necessary work is to transform the individual consciousness's negative energy into positive energy. The antidote for hate is love. The Minute Meditation practice (chapter 13) may manifest the antidote. Try it!

HATE - FORGIVING

Hate is a strong negative emotion. It is the misuse of your purest vibrating energy. It is an obstruction to forgiveness.

When someone has harmed you in your life or work situation, you may easily get caught up in a strong dislike for the individual or situation. The problem is, if the strong dislike is allowed to fester, it manifests as hate in every pore of your mental and physical consciousness. This causes intense resentment, discontent, withdrawal, anger, and a desire for revenge – consciously or unconsciously.

When it is difficult to forgive, you are in the claws of hate – hating a situation or individual who has caused harm. In doing so, you deprive yourself of the freedom only forgiving "gives you."

Hate may cause resistance to forgiving. At the mental state of consciousness, you may be stuck with a false belief that *not* forgiving is a way of punishing the one who has caused the hurt. Remember, the individual who has caused the harm, in ignorance, has probably moved on without you in mind. The grudge you hold is holding on to you, not to anyone else. It affects your life, your well-being, and your spiritual progress.

Hate influences your thinking and decision-making and affects your health. Hate is not an emotion to be ignored. The danger is that the longer you harbor such a strong emotion, the more comfortable you may become with it, to the point where letting it go becomes a struggle.

Is it easy to forgive? No, it is not. Why not? It is not easy because while you are in the mental state of consciousness, memory constantly rises to remind you of the pain and hurt, recreating it repeatedly.

Is it possible to forgive? Yes. Why? It is possible because forgiveness is loving at the higher state of consciousness. This is the natural state of your divinity, which is beyond the mental - memory state. To forgive *is* divine, and you *are* a "Divine being."

Yes, you do continue to have feelings in the mental state of consciousness, but your work is to be aware of a rising feeling and not accept it personally. In your spirituality, there is no person; never has been, never will be. While a person seems to appear on this earth plane, your greater spirituality is that of the One Consciousness. Realize the armor of your spirituality, and no one or thing can penetrate who and what you are.

Hate does not exist in the source of your being. Consequently, yours *is* a forgiving nature. Your work is to rise above any feeling of discomfort.

The one who has caused harm is a blessing in disguise because you are given the opportunity to express forgiveness. How else could you ever express it? It is a responsibility and privilege to grant forgiveness.

You are the one who most benefits from the opportunity to forgive. When you have the opportunity to forgive, you have the opportunity to progress spiritually by leaps and bounds. Be grateful for the blessings that are bestowed up-on you when given the opportunity to express forgiveness.

In truth, there is always only the "One." Thus, in forgiving others, you always forgive yourself. Hate dissolved in the reservoir of forgiveness is to realize a peace grounded in love and the Oneness of your God Being.

Hate and Love – *Same Energy*

Hate is a negative emotion usually ex-pressed with anger and fear. Hate is an emo-tion that is usually ignored when discussing climate change. However, since hate and love are expressed on this plane of opposites, dis-cussing both has its benefits. You could say hate and positive energy are the opposite sides of the same coin, except that energy has no sides. Therefore, the same vibrating energy expressed as hate (negative), once purified, may be expressed as love (positive).

You may be aware of the power of love. Imagine this same power used as hate. There is no stronger emotion than hate expressed in anger and fear that can devastate the mind, body, and environment.

What you send out (give) returns to you multiplied many times. Vibrating energy is vibrating energy. It may be used/expressed and reused/re-expressed. If you misuse it, you are responsible for cleaning it up, and it is as good as new (chapter 14). Any negative vibrating energy expression may be transformed into a silent Instant of purification/forgiveness (*The Minute Meditation, It Is Profound! Book 2: Workbook*, Topic 99: A Silent Instant).

12

SPIRITUAL
CENTER

I promised you a review of your Spiritual Center. The purpose of the review is to give you an understanding of the importance of your Spiritual Center and what role it plays in the realization of the three-sided climate change issue and the One Consciousness. I will admit that this is not an easy one to immediately grasp. If, however, you practice the Minute Meditation (chapter 14), you may appreciate your Spiritual Center's existence and value. So, here we go!

There is a spiritual center (not an object or feeling you experience) at the center of the chest between the breasts. It is referred to as the Spiritual Center and the 4th Chakra. The Spiritual Center is where you may realize the One Consciousness. It is where you may be blessed with the realization of your spirituality. As you are aware of the Spiritual Center area, you may come to the One Consciousness, where a purer, finer vibrating energy may be realized

On this earth plane, your footsteps have but one purpose — to take you to the One Consciousness and the Oneness of your God in spirit and truth. Your Spiritual Center is the access door to your spirituality. It is through the

Spiritual Center that you may seek to realize your Oneness with all humanity and the environment. Your soul and mind devoted to the love of your God will guide your footsteps into an expanded Spiritual Center.

Within your Spiritual Center, truth may be revealed through the One Consciousness and translated with a purified mind. All mystical mysteries are resolved here, and knowledge, understanding, and wisdom are realized. Here you may realize your uniqueness – and the importance of climate change.

With an expanded Spiritual Center, your form may be filled with the grace of unconditional love. Within your Spiritual Center, you are taken on a mystical journey where you are not alone, never have been, and never can be (*The Minute Meditation, It is Profound! Book 5: The Three of You – You Are Never Alone*). The Minute Meditation may guide you directly to your Spiritual Center, the One Consciousness – your unbroken connection to the environment and the spirituality of your being. Trust the Minute Meditation is a direct path.

13

THE
MINUTE MEDITATION
Direct Path

The Spiritual Center is where revelations and realizations are born. The Minute Meditation's teaching direction may take you straight to your Spiritual Center and gratitude for your environment. There is no extraneous dialogue and no stringent guidelines. There are no hindrances of any kind between you and the realization of your spirituality.

The Minute Meditation is for you who are interested in the present "now." It is for you who are interested in meditation without mental or verbal words, in solitude, simplicity, and silence. Do not separate your silent inner practice from your outer practical living. All are spiritual activities. Washing dishes and scrubbing floors are spiritual activities when you do them with conscious awareness.

When you learn the Minute Meditation practice and maintain it with a determined purpose, you may progress. It is a silent meditation practice that may open your Spiritual Center. You cannot separate yourself from the spirituality of your being. With the Minute Meditation, you may come to realize the value of your environment and the connection it has with your God essence.

14

THE
PRACTICE

The Minute Meditation practice is a time set aside to witness the inner rising of the mind's content and beyond. It is a practice of inner silence, and as you faithfully practice, you may gradually awaken to the realization of your relationship with your environment.

The Minute Meditation practice guides you to the entrance door of your inner life. It may bring you to the realization of the present and a life lived in the present. The hurts, sufferings, and emotional pain of this world may be purified and healed when you can live in the present with other beings and your environment.

The Practice:

1. Sit comfortably on a chair or couch or on a cushion on the floor. Close your eyes, and rest your hands on your lap.

2. Slowly inhale deeply and slowly exhale, relaxing your entire body. Continue to breathe normally.

3. Consciously become aware of your Spiritual Center *area* (center of the chest, between the breasts) and rest with the awareness

of your Spiritual Center *area.* If thoughts, images, or sensations arise, do not dialogue, converse, engage, or respond to their rising (your attention is already there). Instead, allow them to rise and, again, gently become aware of your Spiritual Center.

~~

Is that not easy enough? Nothing complicated here. There are no obstacles between you and your Spiritual Center. Continue the Minute Meditation practice as follows. No matter how often thoughts, emotions, or any of the senses arise, gently become aware of your Spiritual Center again.

You are *not* to focus on the Spiritual Center or attempt to still the mind. There is nothing to feel. You are resting with awareness of your Spiritual Center *area.* Do *not* label any of the rising thoughts, emotions, or senses. For example, when a bird sings, all that is occurring is a rise in the sense of hearing. The identity "bird" is a conditioning label; do not use it.

At the end of your silent practice period, take a few moments to become consciously aware of your mental and physical senses before returning to regular activity. Practice the Minute Meditation at any time before a meal, at least two hours after, and about an hour after liquid juices. The changing energy vibration will interfere with the digestion process. Water is fine.

Start your silent meditation practice with one minute twice a day. Allow the practice time to extend naturally. Be consistent. Practice twice a day.

If, for any reason, you find it challenging to become aware of the Spiritual Center *area*, place your hand on the Spiritual Center *area* for the first few minutes of the meditation practice. Be patient with your practice. There is no hurry. Allow the practice to gradually give rest to a restless mind. Accept that no one is rushing you.

Trust that the bumps on the way will smooth out as your practice wears them down. Every moment you practice the Minute Meditation helps to smooth out a rough spot. The Minute Meditation practice allows for time out and rests as it moves you on either slowly or rapidly, according to your devotional determination. Keep in mind that as you practice the Minute Meditation, it moves directly to one place: from a resting mind to your Spiritual Center.

15

MEDITATION SUPPORTERS
Helpful Suggestions

The following are a few helpful suggestions for your meditation practice on your spiritual journey. Work with the ones that are most comfortable for your practice.

SITTING

Sitting is the usual position taken during a silent meditation practice. Sitting may be in a comfortable chair or on the floor. If you are practicing sitting on a chair, you may choose to use an armless chair for safety. Keep your head and chin relaxed and your hands on your lap. If you wish, you may use a shawl. The purpose of a shawl is to allow you to turn within more easily.

Sitting in the same area of your home or place of practice may help you feel more comfortable with your practice. However, the practice may be done anywhere where your safety is not at risk. Sit still during your practice. If discomfort rises, slowly and quietly adjust your posture. Any movement while you are practicing should be performed in slow motion. The less you disturb your vibrating energy, the better.

If you wish to stop your practice, stop. Do not force yourself to practice any length of time. Allow the time you practice to increase naturally. Be patient and gentle with your silent practice. Your determined purpose of sitting will form the sitting habit and allow you to practice more easily. At the end of your practice, give yourself a moment to readjust to your immediate environment. Always get up carefully and slowly from your practicing position.

You are always encouraged to practice in a sitting position. If, for health reasons, you are not able to sit, then, of course, lie down. However, guard against falling asleep. Remember, a fool goes to sleep, and a fool wakes up. You are practicing a silent meditation to wake up, not to take a nap.

TOOLS

Tools are aids on your spiritual path that can assist you. Books, tapes, teachings, stories, symbols, and rituals are tools. Those are some of the many tools of various kinds. What is considered sacred to you may not be to another. Although you may respect all available tools, it is your belief in any one tool that matters.

Metaphysical Scriptures, books, tapes, and films may help guide you along your spiritual path. All tools serve to help your spiritual progress. However, some may be more or less useful at different stages of your practice.

Tools should be approached with contemplative reverence. However, tools are about truth, not truth itself. Truth is who and what you are. It is not outside of you. It is within you.

Use whatever tool/s that you are drawn to and believe may help. Guard against becoming attached to any tool. It is as if you have taken a boat to cross a river; once there, you do not carry the boat around on your head. You leave it for someone else to use.

Be grateful for any tool's use. When you are finished with it, leave it behind and move on. The critical thing to remember is that you never use any tool while practicing meditation. Mixing your practice with any tool or practice will stall your spiritual progress. Do not do it. Your inner guidance needs no tool and can teach you all things directly.

FLEXIBILITY

Flexibility gives you the freedom to adjust, correct, reconsider, and change. When you begin a new silent practice, you may find being flexible is difficult. You may have been taught to be consistent with your practice time and place. However, that may not always be possible.

Once your time and place are established, making even a temporary change may be met with resistance. An active lifestyle may require flexibility at any time. Be prepared to adjust to new surroundings and accept the changes as they may occur.

There are times when you must adjust to a new routine. Being flexible will give you the ability to adapt your practice whenever and wherever necessary. Do not sacrifice your practice in the fires of temptation.

If you are not flexible, traveling for a time to a strange environment could cause an interruption of your practice. Do not trouble yourself with the outer appearances of change in your life. All too often, you may become attached to a particular time, place, or sitting cushion. You want everything to be the same—nothing out of order. In most situations, that would be ideal. As a dedicated truth student, you must be flexible enough to adjust to a moment of change as it presents itself.

The Minute Meditation practice is a direct path to your Spiritual Center. You are never locked into a rigid position on the path. Spiritual growth causes changes and requires flexibility to adjust and accept changes as they occur.

TIME

Time is relative to this plane of opposites. When you first begin a silent meditation practice, you begin with one minute twice daily. It is unnecessary to intentionally place strict time limits on your silent practice. Allow your practice to expand.

This allows your mind and body to adjust to sitting naturally. You do not want to judge any of your practice periods by their length. Longer is not better, nor is shorter worse. The important point is to practice twice a day. One minute is an eternity in the silence.

Your sitting will eventually become a habit. The time necessary for your practice will become established and comfortable. There is never a need to force your practice time. If you are restless or uncomfortable, get up and return to the practice at another time when you are at ease.

The fruit of your practice will be experienced in your daily life as you can respond to the needs of others and your own legitimate needs. A silent meditation practice time need not be dreaded, nor should it be forced. Your practice will meet your needs in its own time. Relax and let the practice *do you*. Time, place, cushions, and shawls may be helpful tools, but all you ever need to practice the Minute Meditation is *"you."*

16

COURAGE
Being Brave

You might think courage (being brave) isn't necessary for the Minute Meditation practice. However, it often takes courage to begin and maintain a Minute Meditation practice. At the beginning of a change of mind, one travels by courage. You may often be challenged. There is always the force of others and situations to distract you from your intent.

You are courageous when you are willing to surrender with unwavering faith to the inner guidance of your Spiritual Center. It takes courage to express gratitude for the environment. There may be many times during a Minute Meditation practice when you must rely on your inner strength to continue. Standing firm during difficult times may require all the courage you can muster.

As you come to realize the truth, your life tends to change, and those around you aren't always receptive to the change. It may take courage to accept what others cannot. When you realize the life of the environment depends on your thoughts, words, and actions, it may require courage to continue.

The Minute Meditation practice may threaten relationships. You may feel threatened by the prospect of giving up something or someone; therefore, there may be pressure on you to give up your practice. On the other hand, courage may hold you steady in your resolve to protect the environment. All around you, there may be the temptation to please others, to take an easier path, a more familiar one. Stepping out of your comfort zone may require courage of the highest order.

To accept all you are given and live out of truth takes courage never before known. To do otherwise is to insult your spiritual integrity and deny the spirituality of your being. When you realize your spirituality, your consciousness changes, and the climate changes are positive. Less negativity means fewer disasters.

It takes courage to change your position on climate change to a positive one. It takes courage to admit that you were part of the problem. It even takes courage to announce that you intend to be part of the solution. Yes, it takes courage to be a leader.

17

A LEADER

Be One!

Peace between you and the climate change deniers begins with peace within you. The Minute Meditation practice may help you achieve that peace. A peaceful you is a powerful attraction. A peaceful, selfless leader is a blessing with compassion, clarity, and discernment. As you practice the Minute Meditation, discernment may rise from the fertile ground of your Spiritual Center.

Discernment

Discernment is the understanding of the differences in a situation or circumstance as they appear. Discernment pierces the truth of evil intent toward climate change. Discernment considers the entire field of preferences. Like a sponge, it absorbs all and does not judge or condemn. Discernment is aware of the necessary decision to be reached and brings a quick resolution, solution, or conclusion to any of life's crises. Therefore, discernment plays a significant role in climate change decision-making, as does communication.

Communication

A great leader understands the art of communication. However, a good communicator does not express their views on the edge of a sword. Ours is a world of mixed humanity. Because of the seemingly complex scheme of things, you cannot drag others along, kicking and screaming. The Minute Meditation practice taps into the simplicity of what we all have in common—our desire to be loved, accepted, *and* understood.

~~

Bob and Alex are calmly enjoying a walk on the beach on a sunny, warm day. The ocean is inviting them to ride its waves.

"Let's go for a morning swim," fun-loving Alex says.

"Oh no," a fearful Bob replies. *"Yesterday, George saw an alligator near the shore."*

"An alligator! He is nuts. There are no alligators in the ocean. He must have seen a shark."

Ah! Relieved, Bob figures, *"Maybe the shark ate the alligator."*

"No, no," insists Alex with a touch of impatience, *"there are no alligators in the ocean."*

Bob reasons, *"That's because the shark ate it."*

With a face contorted with frustration, Alex is about to lose it.

"What is wrong with you? I never said the shark ate the alligator. I said Bob must have seen a shark."

"It must have been after the shark ate the alligator," Bob insists.

Sparked by irritation, Alex loses it. *"Hell, I cannot talk with you. You do not listen. Go for a swim, and maybe the alligator will eat you."*

"So, it's still out there?"

Alex, spewing like the mouth of a volcano, stomps off, yelling,

"I give up. You are impossible."

~~

A separation between Alex and Bob yawns wider with each attempt to communicate. Why? Each heard what he *wanted* and responded to what he *thought* he heard. The expectation, of course, was that each understood the same meaning the words carried. The more they spoke (communicated), the more they shut themselves off from each other.

When communicating, it helps to understand where the other is coming from and where they hope to go. Pauses and moments of silence allow this approach to move along smoothly. The art of communicating can be an arduous effort, yet the awesomeness of its accomplishment is a treasure more significant than the accumulation of titles or riches.

Raising your voice or stomping your feet is not a helpful tool in communication. With a quiet tone and sensitive prodding, minds are changed, and a helping hand is extended. It is about finding ways to gently bring others along a path they are not familiar with. Individuals' minds will make a difference. You and others can cure the worst climate-change infection, which harms everyone's health.

Some will ridicule or challenge a leader's dedication. There is always someone to criticize. Unfortunately, criticizing has a way of eliciting fault. For many individuals, organizations, and politicians, criticizing has become an art form. It is not about to end in your lifetime.

Through all the ups and downs, your dedication will carry you past the drama, complaints, *and* criticism. When you are worn, tired, and disturbed by disappointments of this world's lack of response to the environment's needs, that's when your dedication kicks in. It reminds you why you are dedicated and what your purpose is: saving your life and the life of the planet. During the darkest of times and against all the odds, you refuse to give up. That is what a leader does!

It's during these times that a residue from conditioned doubts and temptations may rise to thwart your creative abilities. Having an established Minute Meditation practice (chapter 14) may make a difference. Being a leader in an unpopular position is not the most comfortable place to be.

Doubts and temptations may test you. There are no greater obstacles or hindrances to a leader than the ever-present, haunting doubts. They come from every direction at the most unexpected time.

Doubts

Doubts trigger a chain reaction of disbelief, wavering, distrust, and a lack of creativity that may slow your progress on positive climate change. Doubts have neither integrity nor respect for a positive leader. Doubts attack your self-esteem, threaten your sanity, and will do anything to distract you. Doubts have no sense of proportion. As a result, you may have doubts about whether to stop, stay, or go forward.

Doubts may nag you for having the audacity to be so bold. There are doubts when there is no progress, and doubts when you *are* making progress. They will linger as long as possible. With doubts, it is always a lose-lose situation. So, take doubts seriously as you would temptations.

Temptations

As for temptations, they want something you have: dedicated leadership. For all practical purposes, temptations hold hands with doubts. The goal is the same – to distract you from your intended purpose.

Temptations will be as attractive as possible and make all the noise necessary to grab your attention. You are not immune to the temptations of this world. Temptations want you to move in their direction.

Once you make a decision, a temptation will attack you with whatever is necessary to keep you from doing your work as a leader. Temptations are smooth talkers and polite. But beware, temptations do not play fair. Temptations are always offering something, someplace, or someone to interfere. So, be vigilant of the attractions that temptations will offer to take away your climate change leadership.

The rightness of temptations' offerings is known by the direction temptations would take you. In either case, doubts or temptations may become a detour, tempting you to take a plan in the opposite direction. The thing to remember about doubts and temptations when they arise is not to indulge in a dialogue (chapter 14) with either one. Be a calm presence and a listening ear, and be willing to work with others. You will quickly find that what you expect of others is expected of you. You are not greater than those you serve. Inherent in a leader's nature is to serve all, including climate change.

Great things are accomplished not by thinking of limits but by doing great things without hesitation.

Hesitation

Hesitation is a moment of indecision. He who hesitates is confused. Hesitation stalls your willingness to serve and holds you in a place of fear of going backward *or* forward. Hesitation involves mixed emotions, which may stir fear about doing what is necessary.

Hesitation is not a lack of trust; it's a misplaced trust in a personal sense of failure. In a moment of hesitation, you may act as a judge and jury prepared to pass a guilty sentence for your actions. The fear of not pleasing others and of bearing guilt over anticipated failure may contribute to your stalling and to continually repeating the same old arguments about climate change, with its pros and cons. It is at a tremendous cost to you and the environment's physical well-being.

This world is full of good and kind people with beautiful minds. It is also riddled with closed minds. Don't be dismayed by the individuals who are not prepared to follow.

The beneficial change manifesting from your expression of consciousness is the best testimonial and the most seductive persuasion for others to follow. The purity of the mind is the elixir that turns minds of steel to pure gold, a gold that softens and changes minds.

We are more alike than not! We all want good health and an environment that supports it. A great historical movement did not occur by holding back the tide of a much-needed leader, a leader who sought neither self-gratification nor self-recognition. The environment is constantly aware of the service it receives from the resources it provides.

Others may pressure you to stay *your* course and allow climate change to fend for itself. Your best communication skills will be needed because the old always has a way of clashing with the new. Newness takes a little getting used to. However, steadfastness will help keep you focused on your intended goal.

Communication can be a daunting task because of the different states of individual consciousness. If you are like Alex, the temptation will be to say, "The hell with you," and walk away. That would be the easiest action to take, but don't look for the easy. Instead, be prepared to do the difficult.

There isn't a more significant task that would honor yourself and your fellow human beings more than caring about climate change. Because climate change affects the environment, it touches everyone's life in one way or another. You can be a leader who protects *your* physical and mental health and helps restore the environment from climate change. Giving up a minute twice a day may not be at the top of most individuals' lists of things to do. Will you put it at the top of your list? Will you, do it? Are you game? Are you up for it?

Accept the Minute Meditation challenge of one minute twice daily for eight weeks. Make it a lifetime practice. It's easy. It's simple. It may change your life. So, share it with your family, friends, and the rest of Mama Earth's kids. Change your consciousness, change your life, and help climate change to preserve a healthy, vibrant environment.

18

REFLECTION
Inner Moral Sense

A farmer had two horses. He always complained to his neighbor that he could not tell them apart. Finally, his weary neighbor came up with a solution.

Raising his hand in a gesture of warm reassurance, he suggested, *"Just measure them, and perhaps there is a difference that will help you to tell them apart."*

"Good idea," thought the appreciative farmer as he hurriedly retrieved a measuring stick. The following day, his neighbor anxiously inquired,

"Well, did it help?"

The astonished farmer gleefully reported, *"Yeah, sure enough, it did. The white one is six inches taller than the black one."*

~~

You can be like the farmer and not notice the obvious (climate change). Or, better yet, you can read on and see the obvious. Do you remember Abraham Lincoln, Gandhi, and Mother Teresa? Each was the power of one who made a difference in the lives of many. Each was an individual who cared about the whole of humankind. They cared enough to do something.

And what about Oprah or Bill Gates? They cared enough to make a difference in the lives of many. You are the same. You are the power of one who can see what is happening to the climate and the health of the environment. You are the power of one who can start with yourself and ultimately make a difference.

Scientists, environmentalists, the media, and the United States EPA offer comprehensive data on climate change and health-related diseases. From the air and water to the delicate balance of the ecosystem, the news is a mix of good and bad. Media overexposure is not getting the message through. Let's face it: fear, threats, hell, and damnation sermons are not very popular or practical anymore. Anyway, they have been tried and retried. Unfortunately, you can only take so much bad news before you dim your sight, close your ears, and shut down.

It's easier to turn away from bad news, especially when the topic is about the perils of climate change. Short of someone setting your hair on fire, getting your attention is becoming more complex. The quickest way to turn you off is to repeat the endless climate change warning statistics and catastrophic predictions. If they had ever worked, the environment would not be withering away.

First, there must come an individual with a change of consciousness. Simply put, do you want a healthy mind and body? Without a healthy planet, neither is possible. *It is*, after all, about *you*: *your* physical health, *your* mental health, and *your* total well-being.

Your health will suffer from the thoughtless disregard of the environment's resources. Denial of climate change and an imbalance created over hundreds of years of environmental use and abuse reflects individual consciousness. Turning your back on the environment is tantamount to ignoring your expression of consciousness.

Accepting and respecting your expression of consciousness opens the possibility of leadership where it is missing and action where necessary. This is because the universe exists within consciousness. Therefore, all that exists in the universe exists within consciousness.

To have a healthy you and a clean, abundant, productive environment, the work must begin with your consciousness. Consciousness is vibrating energy, moving from an inner to an outer expression. So to maintain a healthy balance in the outer world, there must first be a healthy balance within your consciousness, your vibrating energy.

Understanding the power of your consciousness will help you comply with the laws of the universe. Just think what you and millions like you could do to improve health conditions and an ailing environment. It is the power of *one multiplied* a millionfold.

The outer world conforms to the inner, not the other way around. You have an inner power that may pierce the illusion of an inner-outer separation. It is the power of one. The environment reflects your inner individual moral sense. It is not separation. It is a reflection.

Even during your most despicable behavior toward the environment, it unconditionally provides for you. Against all the odds, the environment attempts to meet your demands. Should you not demand the same of yourself that you demand of the environment?

Should you not be expected to put out as much effort in maintaining the earth as you expect it to put out for you? If you cannot honestly answer these two questions, not to worry. The answers and the "how to" are provided. Yes, there are all kinds of thoughtful strategies suggested.

Suggested strategies:
· Conserve
· Ocean Care
· Plant trees
· Wetland protection
· Beach nourishment
· Water conservation
· Community Recycling
· Preserve the wilderness
· Improve energy efficiency
· Protect natural ecosystems
· Control population explosion
· Cut greenhouse gas emissions
· Regulate logging in the rainforest
· Utilize coastal protection methods

~~

They all seem great, don't they? Perhaps you could add to the list. The problem is that they all begin with outer activities. So, how many do you think are getting done? Better yet, how many individuals do you believe, including yourself, are actively and continuously involved with any one or more of these strategies? Are you using one hand to count on? Sad.

Of course, outer work should be included. However, if inner work is excluded, outer work does not get done. So how does it all get put together? From where is the much-needed help going to come? Can technology help? Can science help? Can *God* help? God didn't create the mess; individuals did.

Your senses—seeing, hearing, touching, tasting, and smelling—are used to experience the world's environment. The experiences may be the most pleasurable extraction of all that the world has to offer. It is all at your disposal to take and enjoy. However, the planet *will* hold you responsible for excesses, overindulgence, and abuse.

The best time to recognize that you have a role in the ecology of your inner consciousness and outer environment is today. Playing the waiting game is only a disastrous stall. Waiting cuts into creativity and ingenuity and prolongs the pain and suffering for you and the environment. Waiting for an opportunity, the right moment, or for others to act first is a waste of time.

Waiting creates an imaginary future holding pattern. Whenever you are waiting for others to act, you are in a dead zone, a mental freeze. Therefore, it is better to accept, allow, and respect the choices and decisions others make for themselves, so you can get on with the work that *begins with you.*

Accept:

Acceptance of others frees you from judging.

When you accept others, you are accepting yourself, and that acceptance is an expression of self-love.

Acceptance of any given moment may reveal the present conditions.

Allow:

When you allow others to be where they are, your expectations, stress, and struggles are significantly reduced.

You will lose fewer friends if you allow and are patient with those who are not of the same mind. You cannot drag others along with you. Giving up criticizing those who have different views from yours may deepen your own commitment.

Respect:

Honor others with the same respect you believe you deserve. This contributes to a positive state of mind.

Respect for yourself and others may bring about compromise.

When you respect others' beliefs, you suffer less from emotional turmoil.

~~

The above are a few benefits of accepting, allowing, and respecting others' different views. The benefits allow you to move along. Converting others is not your responsibility. However, you can convert yourself and enjoy the benefits.

The environment is in intensive care. It's fighting for its life, *your* life. When the near death of the environment is the near death of you, it is time to realize that the environment's needs *and* your needs depend on each other.

CONCLUSION
One Side

Now you are aware of the cause of climate change: consciousness, yours and mine. You are also aware that climate change affects the environment, and it is the responsibility of each of us and all of us together. Although it appears to be a three-sided issue, only one side is necessary: a healthy, vibrant environment.

We are individual expressions of the One Consciousness, never separate from one another or from our environment. All are in the One Consciousness. All manifest within the One Consciousness, including the environment.

A negative climate change is an expression of our consciousness. We change it for good or for bad, and we shall suffer the consequences when we cause climate change that harms our environment. We harm the environment; we harm ourselves.

To stop negative climate change, we must change consciousness. A change of consciousness is the only solution to the change of minds that can realize the environment is a gift not to be abused, misused, or neglected. It is a gift of love.

Remember the two questions I asked you at the beginning? Do you want a healthier life? Do you want a more stress-free life? Well, now you may understand how you may have both. You can practice the Minute Meditation (chapter 14) and make a climate change difference. Your health and the planet will be grateful.

BIBLIOGRAPHY

Warming: Opposing Viewpoints. San Diego CA: Greenhaven Press, Inc, 1997.

Yehuda Berg, *Kabbalah on Green: Consciousness and the Environment*. New York: The Kabbalah Centre, 2008.

Harold W. Bernard, Jr., *Global Warming Unchecked*. Bloomington and Indianapolis: Indiana University Press, 1993.

Gale Christianson E., *Greenhouse: The 200-Year Story of Global Warming*. New York: Walker Publishing Co, Inc., 1999.

Carla Mancari, Med, *Eco-You, A Power of One, Improve Your Health, Improve Your Life*. Celestial Literary Group, 1997.

Carla Mancari, MEd, *The Minute Meditation, It is Profound! Book 2: Workbook*. The Celestial Literary Group, 2017.

Carla Mancari, MEd, *The Minute Meditation, It is Profound! Book 5 The Three of You, You Are Never Alone.* Celestial Literary Group, 2017.

Lynne Edgerton T., *The Rising TIDE: Global Warming and World Sea Levels.* Washington DC: Island Press, 1991.

Al Gore, *Our Choice: A Plan to Solve the Climate Crisis.* Emmaus, PA: Rodale Inc., Melcher Media, 2009.

George Mitchell J., Senator, *World on Fire: Saving an Endangered Earth.* New York: Charles Scribner's Sons, Macmillan Publishing Company, 1991.

Gerald North, Jurgen Schmandt, and Judith Clarkson, *The Impact of Global Warming on Texas.* Austin, TX: University of Texas Press, 1995.

Michael Oppenheimer and Robert H. Boyle, *Dead Heat.* New York: A New Republic Book, Basic Books, Inc, 1990.

Swami Rama, *Life Here and Hereafter*. Honesdale, PA: Himalayan International Institute of Yoga Science of the U.S.A., 1991.

Justin Worland, *Time,* "The earth faces a climate reckoning. So does the plan to save it," December 25, 2017.

AUTHOR / TRANSLATOR

Carla R. Mancari is an author, translator, life guide, and teacher. She seeks to improve the self-confidence and self-esteem of individuals from all walks of life so that they can meet life's challenges. For more than 45 years, she has guided individuals in understanding life's spiritual principles, activities, and rising emotions in their private and daily lives.

Carla is the recipient of the Christ Consciousness Meditation and the Minute Meditation. Although she had never attended high school and was labeled a retarded child, she attained two University degrees: a B.A. from the University of South Carolina in Columbia, South Carolina, and an MEd from South Carolina State University in Orangeburg, South Carolina. Carla studied at Brigham Young University and attended the School of the Americas in Switzerland.

Carla led a class action lawsuit in the United States Supreme Court to protect minorities' rights (Morton v. Mancari, 1973) and was a certified psychologist. She served in the United States Air Force. Traveling worldwide for many years, Carla studied with Christian,

Hindu, and Buddhist masters. She was a guest on the Larry King Show and a guest lecturer at various colleges, professional groups, book clubs, and at book signings. Carla gained national recognition when featured in *Good Housekeeping*, "The Education of Carla Mancari, 1969." It chronicled her life in 1967-68 when she was the first white woman to receive a Master's degree from the all-Black South Carolina State College in Orangeburg, South Carolina. She is the author of many books. Carla's greatest joy is helping individuals realize their self-worth, unique gifts/talents, and full potential, and wake up to their spiritual reality.

BOOKS

Mancari, Carla R., *The Lessons: How to Understand Spiritual Principles, Spiritual Activities and Rising Emotions, A Comprehensive Collection.* Celestial Literary Group, 2026.

- - - *Christ Consciousness Meditation Practice: Pocket Size.* Celestial Literary Group, 2026.

- - - *Loneliness.* Celestial Literary Group, 2026.

- - - *Racism, Antisemitism+: A Disease of the Mind.* Celestial Literary Group, 2026.

- - - *The Christ Consciousness Meditation Teaching Guide.* Celestial Literary Group, 2026.

- - - *Metaphysical Questions with Answers from the Christ Consciousness.* Celestial Literary Group, 2026.

- - - *When Jesus Is the Guru: A Wayward Christian's Spiritual Walk.* Celestial Literary Group, 2010.

- - - *Eco-You: A Power of One, Improve Your Health, Improve Your Life.* Celestial Literary Group, 2019.

- - - *Walking on the Grass: A White Woman In A Black World.* Celestial Literary Group, 2016.

- - - *Abortion and The Bible: The Abortion Dilemma: A Scriptural Response, A Woman's Spirituality.* Celestial Literary Group, 2017.

- - - *Racism: The Pain of Invisibility.* Celestial Literary Group, 2017.

- - - *The Rising Emotions: Understanding and Mastering Them.* Celestial Literary Group, 2017.

- - - *The Mystical Path: The Serious Student.* Celestial Literary Group, 2017.

- - - *Spiritual Principles: Understanding, Realizing, and Living Them.* Celestial Literary Group, 2018.

- - - *Climate Change: Consciousness Change.* Celestial Literary Group, 2017.

- - - *Words: Locks On The Door or Keys To The Kingdom.* Celestial Literary Group, 2018.

- - - *Aging: Physical to the Mystical.* Celestial Literary Group, 2018.

- - - *Divine Love: Your Nature.* Celestial Literary Group, 2018.

- - - *The Lazarus Rising: The Kundalini – A Rising Dormant Energy.* Celestial Literary Group, 2018.

- - - *Depression: Hopelessness – A Disconnection.* Celestial Literary Group, 2018.

- - - *Jesus Christ: Teacher.* Celestial Literary Group, 2018.

- - - *The Mystical Surrender: Giving In.* Celestial Literary Group, 2018.

- - - *Death Ain't Dead: Empty Graves.* Celestial Literary Group, 2018.

- - - *Common Decency: Your DNA.* Celestial Literary Group, 2018.

- - - *Christians?: Common Decency.* Celestial Literary Group, 2018.

- - - *Beyond Buddhism: Meditations.* Celestial Literary Group, 2018.

- - - *Exit: Get Ready, Set, Go.* Celestial Literary Group, 2018.

- - - *Meditation: Good For You.* Celestial Literary Group, 2018.

- - - *How To Love "You": Begins with You.* Celestial Literary Group, 2018.

- - - *Consciousness: Yours.* Celestial Literary Group, 2018.

- - - *Suicide: Understanding It.* Celestial Literary Group, 2018.

- - - *Detachment: Realizations.* Celestial Literary Group, 2018.

- - - *Detachment: Christian.* Celestial Literary Group, 2018.

- - - *Sexual Abuse By The Church – Its Root, Coerced Celibacy.* Celestial Literary Group, 2018.

- - - *Guns and Guts: The Courage To Act.* Celestial Literary Group, 2018.

- - - *Jesus, The Way: A Mystical Understanding.* Celestial Literary Group, 2019.

- - - *Motivation: Self-Motivated.* Celestial Literary Group, 2019.

- - - *Totally Free: Is Killing Me.* Celestial Literary, Group, 2018.

- - - *A 30-Second Meditation For Teenagers.* Celestial Literary Group, 2018.

- - - *A 30-Second Meditation For Seniors.* Celestial Literary Group, 2017.

- - - *The Five Faces Of Love.* Celestial Literary Group, 2019.

- - - *Angel In The House.* Celestial Literary Group, 2019 (A Children's Book).

- - - *Put It In The Bible: Prayerful Requests.* Celestial Literary Group, 2019.

- - - *Hate: A Dark Emotion.* Celestial Literary Group, 2019.

- - - *Greed: It's Addictive.* Celestial Literary Group, 2019.

- - - *On Being Young: Choices.* Celestial Literary Group, 2019.

- - - *Gratitude: Expressed, Sincere.* Celestial Literary Group, 2019.

- - - *Humor: A Necessity.* Celestial Literary Group, 2019.

- - - *A Christian: Are You One?* Celestial Literary Group, 2019.

- - - *Habit: How To Switch Meditation Practices.* Celestial Literary Group, 2019.

- - - *Impeachment: Living On The Dark Side.* Celestial Literary Group, 2019.

- - - *The Jesus I Know.* Celestial Literary Group, 2019.

- - - *Grace: Spirit And Truth.* Celestial Literary Group, 2019.

- - - *Temptation.* Celestial Literary Group, 2019.

- - - *The Christian Journey: Teacher Student Relationship.* Celestial Literary Group, 2019.

- - - *The Beloved: Who Is The Beloved?* Celestial Literary Group, 2019.

- - - *What Now, Lord? Enlightenment.* Celestial Literary Group, 2019.

- - - *What If I Were Gay?* Celestial Literary Group, 2019.

- - - *Mother Mary: Mother of Jesus.* Celestial Literary Group, 2019.

- - - *I Remember America.* Celestial Literary Group, 2019.

- - - *The Overcoming: Jesus.* Celestial Literary Group, 2019.

- - - *When Faith Is Not Enough.* Celestial Literary Group, 2019.

- - - *The Plane of Opposites: The Work.* Celestial Literary Group, 2020.

- - - *Crisis.* Celestial Literary Group, 2020.

- - - *Grief: Gut-Wrenching Emotion.* Celestial Literary Group, 2020.

- - - *God.* Celestial Literary Group, 2020.

- - - *Regrets: Do You Have Any?* Celestial Literary Group, 2020.

- - - *1968, 1968,1968: The Mind of A Racist.* Celestial Literary Group, 2020.

- - - *Satan.* Celestial Literary Group, 2020.

- - - *Practice Practice: Meditation.* Celestial Literary Group, 2021.

- - - *Christians Without Jesus: Prodigal Son's Journey.* Celestial Literary Group, 2021.

- - - *From Here To There.* Celestial Literary Group, 2021.

- - - *An Awakening Path: Christian Spiritual Principles.* Celestial Literary Group, 2021.

- - - *Holy Scriptures: Uplifting, Inspiring and Comforting.* Celestial Literary Group, 2021.

- - - *Male Female: The Split Soul.* Celestial Literary Group, 2021.

- - - *The Inner Message: Theological Mystical State.* Celestial Literary Group, 2021.

- - - *A Guide To Understanding Mind's Contents And Realizations.* Celestial Literary Group, 2021.

- - - *A Sister's Laughter: Oh! How I Miss It* Celestial Literary Group, 2021.

- - - *Churches: Are They Necessary?* Celestial Literary Group, 2021.

- - - *Metaphysical: Stories and Poems.* Celestial Literary Group, 2021.

- - - *Jesus, Jesus, Jesus.* Celestial Literary Group, 2021.

- - - *The Disciple and The Mystical Guide.* Celestial Literary Group, 2021.

- - - *The Holy Trinity: 1+1+1=1, No Mystery.* Celestial Literary Group, 2021.

- - - *Fear of Jesus: Why?.* Celestial Literary Group, 2021.

- - - *Symbols and Rituals: Christian.* Celestial Literary Group, 2021.

- - - *Christian Minute Meditation.* Celestial Literary Group, 2021.

- - - *Sin!.* Celestial Literary Group, 2021.

- - - *Compassion.* Celestial Literary Group, 2021.

- - - *Silence.* Celestial Literary Group, 2021.

- - - *The Spiritual Zone.* Celestial Literary Group, 2022.

- - - *The Bible Scriptures: Mystical Understanding.* Celestial Literary Group, 2022.

- - - *Lead Us Not Into Temptation: The Lord's Prayer.* Celestial Literary Group, 2022.

- - - *Let's Talk About Jesus, Or Not.* Celestial Literary Group, 2022.

- - - *For The Love of Jesus: Come Back To Your Church.* Celestial Literary Group, 2022.

- - - *Abortion, When Life Does Not Begin! Exodus 21:22-25.* Celestial Literary Group, 2022.

- - - *Morton vs. Mancari: A Plaintiff's Response: How An Average Joe (woman) Landed In The US Supreme Court.* Celestial Literary Group, 2022.

- - - *Christian Spiritual Exercises: The Inner Journey.* Celestial Literary Group, 2023.

- - - *The Kingdom Of God – A Gift.* Celestial Literary Group, 2023.

- - - *An Expression of Love.* Celestial Literary Group, 2023.

- - - *Choices and Decisions On a Spiritual Journey.* Celestial Literary Group, 2024.

- - - *Love Your Enemies: How Can You Do That?.* Celestial Literary Group, 2024.

- - - *Outer Space and Inner Space Travel.* Celestial Literary Group, 2024.

- - - *God – Love: Poets Write About It.* Celestial Literary Group, 2024.

- - - *The Still Small Voice, You Can Hear It.* Celestial Literary Group, 2024.

- - - *The Resurrection: Rising Beyond Body Consciousness.* Celestial Literary Group, 2024.

- - - *Sexual Spiritual Intercourse: Oneness.* Celestial Literary Group, 2024.

- - - *Child Of God: In Spirit and Truth.* Celestial Literary Group, 2024.

- - - *"My Child," Blessed Mother Mary's.* Celestial Literary Group, 2024.

- - - *Strait Gate and Narrow Way: "Few There Be That Find It".* Celestial Literary Group, 2024.

- - - *Strait Gate and Narrow Way: "Few There Be That Find It", Pocket Size.* Celestial Literary Group, 2024.

- - - *The End Of The Beginning, Our Spiritual Journey.* Celestial Literary Group, 2024.

- - - *A Cat Story.* Celestial Literary Group, 2025.

Mancari, Carla. R. *and* **Carpenter, Mary B.** *Scriptural Reference For - The Lessons, A Comprehensive Collection.* Celestial Literary Group, 2026.

- - -*The Minute Meditation, Book 1: It Is Profound!* Celestial Literary Group, 2022.

- - -*The Minute Meditation, Book 2: Workbook, It Is Profound!*. The Celestial Literary Group, 2022.

- - - *The Minute Meditation, It Is Profound! Book 3: The Essentials*. Celestial Literary Group, 2022.

- - - *The Minute Meditation, It Is Profound! Book 4: A Diet For The Soul*. Celestial Literary Group, 2022.

- - - *The Minute Meditation, It Is Profound! Book 5: The Three of You, You Are Never Alone*. Celestial Literary Group, 2022.

- - - *The Minute Meditation, It Is Profound! Book 6: Pocket Size*. Celestial Literary Group, 2022.

- - - *The Minute Meditation, It Is Profound! Book 7 – Teaching Guide*. Celestial Literary Group, 2022.

- - - *The Minute Meditation, It Is Profound! Book 8 – The 4th Chakra*. Celestial Literary Group, 2026.

- - - *Spirituality: Yours*. Celestial Literary Group, 2021.

- - - *Dreams: States of Consciousness*. Celestial Literary Group, 2021.

- - - *A Christian Service With A Silent Christian Meditation*. Celestial Literary Group, 2024.

Casey-Martus, Sandra, and Mancari, Carla R. *The Lessons, How to Understand Spiritual Principles, Spiritual Activities and Rising Emotions, Lessons with Stories Along a Spiritual Journey.* Celestial Literary Group, 2026.

NOTES

www.ingramcontent.com/pod-product-compliance
Lightning Source LLC
Chambersburg PA
CBHW012257240726
48656CB00007B/2425